A BOOK OF EVERYDAY BLESSINGS

"With her characteristic warmth and tenderness, Christine Valters Paintner ushers us into the deep sacredness that permeates our everyday lives, just waiting for us to take notice. These powerful and poetic blessings offer holy accompaniment through every season of life, reminding us of the presence of God in moments both memorable and mundane. This book will be a faithful companion to every spiritual seeker, a luminous guide through the pilgrimages of our lives."

Cameron Bellm

Author of *A Consoling Embrace: Prayers for a Time of Pandemic*

"This is not a book to be read through once and shelved. It is a resource for a lifetime that can help us relish again and again the everyday blessings that present themselves in the quiet, joyful, and challenging periods all of us must travel through. *A Book of Everyday Blessings* creatively opens inner paths we need to find and follow in our spiritual and psychological journey through change. No matter what your background and current situation, I hope you will take a few moments each day to pray with this book. It is, indeed, an everyday blessing."

Robert J. Wicks

Author of *Riding the Dragon*

"There are moments in life—joyful, harrowing, mysterious, and heart-wrenching—when we reach for God, but our words fall short. There are quiet moments, too, when we are tempted to believe our lives too mundane to be infused with God's loving presence. Then, too, our prayer falls silent. But in her new book, Christine Valters Paintner adamantly disagrees, insisting that all moments are worthy of blessing. She reminds us that our God desires that we companion one another through the simple act of blessing, pointing to the good and beautiful even in the humdrum and the challenging. *A Book of Everyday Blessings* gives us new words with which to make holy the ordinary and extraordinary and doggedly insists that God is here, even now, in this suddenly sacred moment. This book will not only provide literal blessings for your everyday journey but also encourage you as you enter times of transition, as you embark on retreat, as you walk with friends and strangers alike, and as you seek out the holy in the world around you. In *A Book of Everyday Blessings*, Paintner has given us a true gift: words to help us name the goodness around us when our own fall short."

Eric A. Clayton
Author of *Finding Peace Here and Now: How Ignatian Spirituality Leads Us to Healing and Wholeness* and *Cannonball Moments: Telling Your Story, Deepening Your Faith*

A BOOK OF EVERYDAY BLESSINGS

100 Prayers for Dancing Monks, Artists, and Pilgrims

CHRISTINE VALTERS PAINTNER

SORIN BOOKS  Notre Dame, IN www.avemariapress.com/sorin-books

Paperback: ISBN-13 978-1-932057-35-5

E-book: ISBN-13 978-1-932057-36-2

Cover and text design by Brianna Dombo Nicholson.

Printed and bound in the United States of America.

Library of Congress Cataloging-in-Publication Data is available.

CONTENTS

BLESSINGS FOR OUR CONNECTION TO THE HOLY WILD

BLESSINGS FOR THE SEASONS

THRESHOLD BLESSINGS

INTRODUCTION

BLESSING THE DAY

Just to be is a blessing. Just to live is holy.
—Rabbi Abraham Joshua Heschel, from "On Prayer"

GOD bless you and keep you,
GOD smile on you and gift you,
GOD look you full in the face and make you prosper.
—Numbers 6:24–26 (translation from *The Message*)

Blessings can be like warm bread for the hungry, a cold drink for those who thirst. Blessings offer hope and encouragement, steep us in gratitude, and nurture our courage. They bring us present to the grace of each moment. The word comes from the Latin, *benedicere*, which means "to speak well of." Blessings help remind us of the love and beauty of the Holy One in our lives and assist us in taking nothing for granted. They act as maps to navigate our human experience, orienting us back to gratefulness and praise.

In Jewish, Islamic, and Celtic traditions, a central practice is to bless the unfolding of the day, each activity, each turning point. Everything becomes worthy of blessing. The Talmud calls for one hundred blessings each day, and through this practice we can shape ourselves into beings who pay close attention and who remember the One from whom all of life flows.

Blessings sustain us in bringing reverence to all of life—from the most ordinary tasks to the great thresholds of our lives. They immerse us in the holy rhythms of the sacred, which are not of our making. In a world obsessed with the scarcity of time, blessings help us to expand each moment like a flower opening its petals on a sunny day. They invite us to breathe more deeply, enlarge our vision, and give honor to our experiences. Blessings help us touch eternity here and now.

A blessing is an acknowledgment of the gifts and graces already present, and using them means that the mundane activities of the day become opportunities to witness grace at work. They become meditations and remembrances.

When my calendar and to-do lists become misplaced holy grails in my life, speaking a blessing is a way to put things back into perspective. When my heart aches and grieves over loss, a blessing is a sanctuary space within which I am held and met by the divine.

St. Benedict wrote in the prologue to his Rule:

> Let us then at last arouse ourselves, even as scripture incites us in the words, "Now is the hour for us to rise from sleep." Let us then, open our eyes to the divine light, and hear with our ears the divine voice as it cries out to us daily. "Today if you hear his voice, do not harden your hearts," and again, "He who has ears to hear, let him hear what the Spirit says to the Churches."

The image of awakening calls us to shake off the slumber that creates a veil between reality and our perception. The act of blessing helps us awaken and see more clearly. When we remember to bless, we consecrate life, whether we are in the kitchen, the office, in church, or standing in a forest. Blessings are incarnational and connect us to the ordinary and everyday rhythms of life. Daily blessings for meals, sleep, and other activities immerse us in a stream of continual gratitude and awe for the divine presence in all things.

Blessings are a threshold between worlds and a portal to God as our source of life. They connect us to our spiritual lineage of saints and ancestors who gave and received blessings themselves. They call us to make our prayers transformative rather than transactional. We pray not just to ask for things but to cultivate a heart of presence and gratitude.

To be a blessing to the world means to hold a sense of profound gratitude for all that is. Blessing has a way of transforming our approach to life into one that is more openhearted, generous, and joyful.

When we bless our actions, we lift up our partnership with the divine in being embodied messengers of healing, love, joy, hope, and more. Receiving a blessing is an act of being seen, witnessed, and loved by another. It weaves us into a community of care and concern.

Blessing is an act of solidarity—it is a way to say to someone, I am praying for you, I am celebrating you, I am grieving with you, and I know the Holy One is praying, celebrating, and grieving with us. To both offer and receive a blessing demands vulnerability so that we can be encountered where we are.

Blessing is *not* about a privileged status over others but about recognizing the blessings we receive, beginning with the gift of life itself, and remembering that in all places and at all moments, we are blessed. We need only shift our perspective. In her poem "It Was Early," Mary Oliver wrote, "Sometimes I need only to stand wherever I am to be blessed" (*Evidence: Poems* [Beacon, 2009], 21).

How This Book Came to Be

I first wrote blessings for our community, Abbey of the Arts, which is a virtual monastery rooted in desert, Celtic, and Benedictine traditions. We have monthly contemplative prayer services and a series of six seven-day prayer cycles on themes like "Earth Monastery," "Monk in the World," and "Soul of a Pilgrim." Many of these prayers began in these gatherings. I sometimes wrote blessings for a retreat I was leading as well. Eventually I started to receive requests to gather these blessings into a book that others could use for their own prayer and reflection, both individual and communal.

I then reached out on social media for suggestions for the kinds of blessings people would love to have, and I received such a great list that guided the writing of many of these prayers. Topics like praying with chronic pain, for a transition, or for someone with dementia moved me deeply, and I spent many hours in prayer, listening for the words that could help to create a mantle of support and protection for those praying them.

Abbey of the Arts is a diverse, ecumenical community made up of people from different Christian denominations and some who have left the church altogether. What we share is a desire for deeply rooted contemplative and creative resources that help us think more expansively about the divine and our place in the world.

These blessings are not written for formal gatherings within particular institutional settings—they are not official Church blessings or intended for particular liturgical rites. Blessings are not reserved for clergy and the ordained but are a practice we are all invited to participate in. When your heart longs to connect your faith with a particular situation in your life, blessings can become a bridge.

They come from an ethos of profound care for suffering and a desire to celebrate life's joys. In this sense, I think they extend across perceived boundaries.

My hope is that this collection reaches beyond our community to meet anyone who yearns for prayers that speak to their longings for inclusivity and justice.

How to Use This Book

This is a book meant to be read, spoken aloud, or even sung if you feel inspired. It can be used for personal prayer but is also encouraged in group settings.

I recommend reading through the titles in the table of contents to see if there is one prayer that shimmers for you or calls to you in some way. Find the page and read it slowly, noticing what longings it stirs in your heart. Feel free to adapt the words to make it more fully fit your situation.

A Note About Language

The ancient monk John Cassian wrote about three renunciations—one of which is our ideas and images of God—so that the Sacred Source can be revealed more fully to us without the blinders of our expectations. I always strive to use inclusive language when talking about God. I also try to be expansive and offer different images to ponder. Even the word *God* can sometimes box us into old ideas.

If any of the names for God I use do not work for you, please feel free to substitute your own image or name for the Holy One. Please also feel free to change the pronouns, depending on whether you are blessing a single person or a group. Make any changes you need to make the blessing more fully your own.

BLESSINGS FOR QUIET MOMENTS

FOR SILENCE AND SOLITUDE

Holy Source of Silence,
beneath the clatter and din of the everyday
you offer your mysteries to our hearts.

You call us to pause,
to slow down and listen to the true longing
planted in each of us by you, a seed of holy desire.

Support us in letting go of the inner and outer noise.
Open wide in us a sacred cave for stillness
where we can attune to your presence.

Enliven us with the gift of your sweet music
and allow us to encounter your holy presence
flaming in each of our hearts.

Help us to catch a note of your song
in the wind or in the voice of another,
in times of sadness, and in the rush of our lives.

In a world so filled with distraction,
we listen for your whispers
that call us to another way of being.
We ask for the courage to respond to all
we discover in this tabernacle of silence.

FOR REST ON THE SABBATH

Sanctifier of Holy Rest,
on the seventh day you paused,
laying
down
the work
of creation,
and entered into sacred stillness.

Let us remember we were freed from slavery
in Egypt and you continue to call us
to be people of liberation.
Kindle in us the strength to say no
to a world of perpetual busyness.
Inspire us to set aside our plans
and goals to receive the lavish gift
of rest for ourselves,
to rediscover the paradise within.

Let the Sabbath be a time of profound renewal,
a gushing forth of the holy well,
a time of intimate connection with you,
and a rekindling of our sacred desires to be of service.
Sustain in us the longing to simply *be*
and not succumb to the demands
of productivity and an endless string of achievements.

Let our lives be a loving witness
to a world of restoration and refreshment
and to the profound goodness of joy and delight
so that we might take pleasure in the generous gift of pausing.

FOR THE GIFT OF REST

Holy One, you call us to the lavish gift of rest.
Support us as we lay aside our tasks, our plans, our worries
and turn to you with open hearts.
Whisper to us in the silence
of your love for us, simply for who we are.

Bless us with the deep renewal
that rest brings and transform our daily patterns
so that we might weave Sabbath into every day.
Slow us down when our minds race,
when our calendars overflow with demands,
when our hearts flutter overwhelmed by life.

Hold us in that holy pause,
reveal to us again the beauty of this world—
of steam rising from coffee,
of the dog's pleading eyes,
of the rose blooming.

Help us to see how everything in creation
takes its time—no rushing, no pushing.
In that open space gather all of our scattered
parts together into the wholeness
of who we were created to be.

FOR BEING PRESENT TO EACH MOMENT

Holy Presence,
guide our gaze back to here and now
and reveal to us that you are with us always.
Awaken us to see each shimmering moment,
each loving gesture, each face full of yearning,
and the ways you dance through creation.
Sustain us in releasing our need to distract
ourselves with things that do not nourish
or that numb us to the possibility of aliveness.

Help us to savor this world
through the gift of our senses
so that each day we look for beauty,
we listen for the music of the world,
we relish our meals,
we inhale the fragrance of flowers,
we feel the embrace of life.

When our attention wanders
to that which depletes us,
gently direct us again to your sacred banquet.

FOR DISCERNMENT

O Holy One,
I stand on a threshold
and seek your grace
to guide me in the direction
of the deepest desires
you have planted in my heart.

Help me to see the abounding signs and synchronicities
that align me with my gifts.
Let me hear your wisdom pouring forth
from soul friends and strangers.
Let me remember the ancient ones
cheering me on from beyond the veil.
May my ancestors bless my path
and my seeking and choosing.

Sophia, Holy Wisdom, bless me
with the capacity to rest
within mystery and unknowing,
to not rush the process,
and to trust in the slow unfolding of truth.
Help me to dwell in the assurance
that there isn't just one way I need to figure out,
but that I am simply called to listen
for the most life-giving option right now
in this season of my life.
Refine my vision so that I can behold
your shimmering presence around me.

Expand my heart
until I see that love is my true call,

and help me to say yes to all
that is in service to you, who is Love.

FOR PEACE

Wondrous Peacemaker,
guide us in a world filled with war,
hatred, and division
to create a place where everyone
can live free from fear of violence.

Care for the soldiers, the victims, the refugees.
Be a balm for their wounds
and guide them to alignment with your holy desires.
Transform the tools of destruction
into vessels of cultivation.

Where bombs rain down,
let tiny seeds sprout among the rubble.
Where the stranger has fled to safety,
let them be welcomed with open arms.
Where the desire for vengeance consumes,
let a new way crack open.

Infuse us with the courage needed
to speak words of care,
to be the presence of peace
in all of our words and actions.

Let the light of your love pulse within us
so that we become bearers of grace.
May the radiance of our dreaming be a sign of hope
so that all might envision together
this more beautiful world.

BLESSINGS FOR DAILY LIVING

FOR A COMPANION ANIMAL

Creator God,
we give thanks for the profound goodness
of our animal companions
and ask for your boundless blessing,
as they bless our lives
with their abiding presence.

They are holy friends coated in fur and fins,
feathers and scales,
wise guides in the way of play and pleasure,
rest and dreams, of seeking snuggles,
who always await us when we are gone.

To know their joy at our return
is a homecoming again and again,
calling us back to our belonging.
This friendship across species and language
enriches our days like nothing else.

May they stay well and thriving
for as long as possible.
May we know this brief span of time
together as the generous gift it is,
a sliver of that original goodness
still echoing through our days.

FOR A SPARK OF JOY ON A BAD DAY

Abiding One,
some days are just hard.
I feel my humanity more keenly,
my edges are raw,
my anxiety flares,
my compassion wanes,
and everything
seems to go from wrong to worse.
Be with me in the ache of this human mess.

Bless this day with clearer vision
so that I might see you pulsing at its heart
and reach for every hand stretched toward me.

Pour out your tenderness,
fill me with hope overflowing for better times,
gift me with the deep rest I need to endure
what feels like so many bad days.

Breathe a spark of joy into me
so that I might resist despair.
Help me to find you near
in the jangle of feelings,
creating a loving space for it all,
for everything is held in your gaze.

FOR GRACE IN THE ORDINARY

Holy One who shimmers even in the mundane,
open my eyes with gratitude for your sustenance
in pipes and plumbing,
in wires and electricity,
in cups of tea and food in the fridge,
in piles of dishes and laundry.
When dullness and boredom visit,
bless all the quiet in-between moments,
the sunlight journeying across the floor.
Help me to see how the most ordinary
is also extraordinary,
how grace dwells
among the bills to pay
and messages that await reply.
Let my shower each morning become a baptism
and my breakfast a communion,
consecrating each act of daily life.
Let my gratitude pour out
in a holy and vibrant yes
for everything quotidian,
to see even this moment as magnificent.

UPON AWAKENING

Bringer of Sunrises,
bless us as we awaken to this new day
with gratitude and a sense of possibility.
Help us to see it as the generous gift it is.

Sustain us as we pause for a while
and open our eyes to wonder and beauty
awaiting us in quiet moments.

Gather into our hearts
the presence of all those in need of prayer
so that we begin this day in a web of kinship and care.

Align our vision with your holy desires
so that we might be the embodied presence
of your love in the world.

If we face challenges ahead,
breathe patience into us and soften our hearts.
Remind us how small gestures are vital,
like kindness and welcome.

Help us to see the hours ahead as gift,
each one a prayer bead, a faceted jewel,
shimmering with your luminous presence.

FOR RELEASE INTO SLEEP

Dream-Bearer, summon me into holy rest
and bless my body as it softens
from aching joints to a tender heart.
Help me release all the tense places
and everything I hold onto from this day.

Breathe into me so that my dry bones
might be renewed this night.
Help me to feel your holy presence
as a sanctuary of sleep,
a tent where I can close my eyes
and be deeply renewed by giving up effort.

I lay down my striving, my grasping,
my longing to make things happen,
anything that feels unresolved,
the worries and fears that grip me,
and descend into the cave of dreams
where the ancient stone meets me as bedrock,
where the darkness becomes a guide
to all that is not visible in the light.

BEFORE ACTS OF SERVICE

God who labors within and through us,
help us bring our full attention
to our work in the world
as we enter into an act of co-creation with you.

Show us all the ways
our work has dignity and purpose,
whether paid or unpaid,
whether it is our heart's true calling
or simply allows us to support ourselves.

Guide us in challenging systems
that exploit and enslave people
through their labor
and help us to build communities
where everyone can thrive by the work of their hands.

Support us in the endeavor to do everything with love,
remembering that each small act of compassion
is woven together into a great tapestry of justice.

Bless our hands as we offer our gifts
in service to your unfolding grace.

FOR CREATIVE JOY

Blessed Source of Joy,
carve out room in us
for the inexpressible delights of love.

Let our hearts become fountains overflowing
into the world with your love and compassion.
Help us to pause each day and whisper, "Thank you,"
for the most ordinary graces and gifts.

In the way that you looked upon your creation
and called everything *so* good, kindle in us
the same generous vision.

Lift us beyond our narrow concerns and help us
to see how there is no separation, that we are all connected.
Support us in honoring our bodies as sacred temples
and losing ourselves in the great cosmic dance.

FOR TRUST IN ABUNDANCE

Spirit of Generous Abundance,
remind us there is always more than enough—
enough food, enough love, enough time, enough resources.
Help us to see how our disconnected patterns of living
amplify our scarcity.

Bring us into the joy and challenge of community
where bread divided multiplies,
where laughter shared overflows.
Empower us to share freely from our own abundance
with others in need. Slow us down to see how time expands
when we breathe and pay attention.

Bless us in our efforts to trust
in your goodness and love pulsing through the world,
sustaining it moment by moment.
Give us the courage to speak out
when resources are distributed unfairly
so that we may remind others there is more to share.

Encourage us to release that which we no longer
need to hold onto so tightly.
Inspire us to live in a way that witnesses
to our trust in the lavish fullness of life.

FOR PATIENCE

Source of Growth and Life,
dazzle us with the rhythm of your seasons
woven into all of creation.
Help us to see how release and rest
are necessary for flowering and fruit.

Bring us reminders each day
of our own holy unfolding,
from waking to working to playing to resting.

Release our grip from calendars and planners,
soften our need to make something happen,
to try to control the outcome,
and reveal your presence arising within us
in a hundred different ways.
Guide our hearts and soften our impatience.

We celebrate this wild grace at work,
in its own time, its own tempo,
inviting us into this sacred dance of trust.

FOR FRIENDSHIP AND COMMUNITY

God of Friendship,
I come to know your love and care
through the embodied presence of others.

Weave me together with kindred spirits,
knit me more closely with friends of the soul,
cultivate in me a kinship with humanity
so that I recognize my struggles and joys in others.

In my loneliness, reveal to me this communion
and may I be a solace to others who ache for connection.
Transform me through conversation and loving presence.

Help me to see how I am part of a great circle
of pilgrims, witnesses, ancestors, and mystics
who guide me to true connection with you.

Gather me into your great wide heart
so that I might discover I am never separate
but always held in love.

FOR STAYING ROOTED IN THE HOLY

Sacred Source of all life,
in the midst of the tumult of our days—
the torrent of terrible news,
the fears we hold for the future,
the ache in our hearts and bodies—
whisper to us words of love
in the breezes rustling the long grass,
in the quiet moment between breaths,
in the kindness of another's eyes.

May this blessing be a balm
and a love note to our hearts
when we feel keenly the pain of the world
and the sorrow of our own losses.

May we see the Holy One as a sacred well
whose waters flow deep below us,
rushing up to bless us and bathe us,
a gushing fountain of refreshment
whenever we pause to listen and be.

May we see the Divine Presence as a holy tree,
roots digging down,
branches abundant with blossoms and fruit,
inviting us to sit and lean against her trunk,
feeling her solid presence along our spines
while life pulses beneath and above us.

Let us reach for the long branches of your love
and bite into the ripe juiciness of your generosity
when we need a reminder of life's sweetness;

let us inhale the fragrant petals of your beauty
when we long for our days to be perfumed.

FOR HOLY FOOLISHNESS

God of Upturned Expectations,
bless us with holy foolishness.

Help us to take ourselves less seriously
and to believe you can accomplish
what we did not think could be done
in impossible situations,
with limited resources,
among injustices demanding rectification,
within traumas needing healing.

Grant us a restless heart
when we witness oppression
and exploitation, hunger and war,
poverty and destruction.

Kindle in us a need to extend our hands
in service to a hurting world,
joining with kindred souls
in communities of care,
knowing ourselves to not be alone.

Help us trust in the tiny seeds we plant,
and may they grow vigorously and flourish.
Let the ripples we send across the waters
of our communities be multiplied by the efforts of others.

Infuse us with courage
to keep loving when it feels hard to love,
to keep being foolish enough
to think we can join with you
in transforming the world.

FOR DEEPER GRATITUDE

Spirit of Generosity,
we come to you with hearts
overflowing with gratitude
for your abundant creation.

As we awaken each morning,
help us to remember
this day is a gift,
this breath is a grace,
this life a wonder.

Remind us
with every flower we see,
every act of kindness,
every moment of connection
to something so much bigger
than ourselves,
to sing out in delight.

Cultivate in us a sense of awe
and trust in your lavish grace.
Let each word of thanks we offer
expand our hearts
until delight inhabits us
and we know love
as our sustenance.

FOR SHELTER AND SAFETY

Sheltering God,
bless those who are without homes,
whether evicted or addicted,
evacuated or fleeing abuse.
Keep them nourished,
warm, and safe,
and guide them to the resources
they need to begin again.

Bless those who are refugees
fleeing their homeland,
bringing only what they can carry.
Comfort the ache of leaving,
inspire courage to board
trucks, boats, and planes
or to keep walking with blistered feet
as they travel into an unknown future.
Let them be greeted with kindness,
welcomed by those who practice
hospitality as a sacred trust,
who know what it is to be an outsider.

Bless the animals left behind
and those abandoned;
may they find their way to new homes.

Open wide the door to our hearts,
remind us of our ancestors fleeing
slavery in Egypt, forty years in the desert,
and of the Holy Family's flight
to escape King Herod's violence.

Help us to see the face of Christ
shimmering in every stranger,
to know we are enriched
each time we extend sanctuary.

FOR CREATIVITY

Spirit of Holy Imagination,
we ask you to bless our vision
with the wisdom to see what is possible.

Help us trust our desire to create
through color, word, shape, gesture, and song.
When our fingers tremble
at picking up a pen or marker,
connect us to the joy of playing
on the white page,
drawing, doodling, dabbling, dreaming,
letting our lives
be a canvas for expression.

When judgments arise
and the inner critic yells,
guide us to hear our intuitions
whispering the way ahead
with quiet confidence.
When our feet feel restless,
inspire us to play music
and dance freely
until peace descends again.

Connect us to the freedom
of making something
for the love of it.
Speak to us in dreams
of what you desire
to create together with us,
making the world
a great work of art.

FOR HOLY BOUNDARIES

Spirit of Protection,
encircle us in every direction;
help us to know
there is nowhere to turn
away from your love.

When life overwhelms,
draw your holy mantle around us
and offer us refuge
from daily demands.
Gift us with quiet moments
of peace and perspective
and help us to stand strong
when our boundaries
are being violated.

Guide us toward
always making more space
for the dreams and desires
you have planted in our hearts,
trusting they have been
given in service to the world.

Empower us to say no
as often as needed,
to remember it as a holy word
that makes room for all
of our sacred yeses.

FOR SUSTENANCE IN DOUBT AND UNCERTAINTY

Holy Mystery,
be with me in my tender places of unknowing,
dwell with me in the cracks of my doubts,
let my uncertainty be a sign of my humility
in the face of your awesome expanse.

Bless me in these sacred gaps
where I release my grasping at answers
and no longer force myself into faith.
Sustain me with clarity over that which is truly vital
and help me to release the rest to wonder.
Hold my hand as I walk through the fog,
seeing only the step in front of me.
Keep my focus on this moment now.

Show me how the soil of my being
is softened by doubts and questions,
creating a fertile ground for future imagining.
Bless this doubt as a doorway,
calling me to release my certainties
and beckoning me to new possibilities
undreamed of until now.

FOR A NEW BEGINNING AFTER DISAPPOINTMENT

Bearer of All Wounds and Ruptures,
bless me in the midst of my disappointment.
Hold my tender, bruised heart gently
as I navigate the loss of a dream,
as I face the emptiness of nothing rather than something.

I had hoped so dearly
for this opportunity, had tasted its sweetness.
In the stripping away I am struggling
with bitterness, with sadness, with longing,
and don't know how to move ahead.

Let me feel the fullness of this loss,
to not negate what I desired
but let it have space
as a reminder of my deepest hopes.

May I feel a kinship now
with those who sit at the edge of their own longing,
anyone who has felt the exposed edges of life.

And when I have let this grief have its place,
bless me with a new dream,
a vision for a new way forward.
Let this disappointment be a doorway
to a new beginning.

FOR CALM IN CHAOS

Loving God,
you care for us as deeply as a mother or father.
Despite trusting in your grace,
I don't feel like I can manage, much less respond,
to all the important events that demand my attention.
Everything in this world aches
for renewal, for a new vision,
for your peaceful and orderly presence.

Navigating life, the news, crisis after crisis—
each day feels like too much.
My heart feels raw and stretched thin,
my throat is choked by tears held back,
my gut is knotted and blocked.

Create a sanctuary for me in your great beating heart;
hold me in compassion and loving care
as I release the torrent of emotion within.

Help me to know that the gifts I carry
are the exact ones the world needs
so that I can let go of everything else
and trust that I am part of a great communion
pulsing on both sides of the veil.

Hold me in the calm of your presence,
steady me with wisdom born of deep time,
of ancient stories of struggle and endurance.
Speak to me through wind and waves,
stone and sunlight, of the peace of simplicity.

Strengthen me to find an anchor within
so that in the chaos and tumult
I am defined by stillness and clarity.
May I become a bearer of love
and a blessing for others in need.

MEAL BLESSING

Source of Sustenance,
bless this food set before us.
Let us remember the many hands that labored
to bring it to our table,
from farmers to field workers,
from transporters to grocery clerks,
to those who prepared and cooked this meal,
a great chain in the sacred work
of satisfying hunger.

We remember the One who sat at table
with all those on the edges
and asked us to break bread together in memory.
May we commit to multiplying our loaves of bread
so that all who hunger are fed.
Bless the conversations between friends
so that we become woven together
in both body and soul.

As we nourish ourselves
with this bounty of delight,
may this food bring us the pleasures
of smell, sight, and taste.
Thank you for feeding us
with the fertility of soil,
the radiance of sunlight,
and the renewal of rain,
for rooting our bodies in the abundance
of a generous Earth.

HOME BLESSING

Loving God,
we ask you to bless this home.
May it be a sanctuary for all who dwell here,
may it be a tabernacle of memories.

We feel this space opening itself wide
and eagerly anticipate our life together here
and the days we will enter with joy,
with longing, with an aching heart,
with dreams both kindled and stripped away.

Let there be much laughter at the table
and meals that nourish body and soul.
Let the walls hold us in our weeping.
Let the bedrooms be a place of rest and retreat,
let the shower refresh us,
let every corner become hallowed.
Let the door be open wide
to welcome in the stranger;
let it also be a secure boundary in times
when safety is needed.
Let sunlight spill through the windows,
blessing our days with radiance.

As we move through each new season,
may our lives unfold slowly
with this home as a place to feel rooted,
and a place from which to lean out into the world
spreading our branches wide.

TO LOVE MORE DEEPLY

Beloved, when you created us,
you celebrated with an exuberant *that's so good*!
Help us to know ourselves as loved,
as formed from love, infused with love,
and made to love.

Expand our hearts with each breath—
with every inhale may we receive love,
with every exhale may we extend love.

May we behold all that is unloved in us
and welcome ourselves home again
to you, the Ground of Love.

May we meet those who are rejected
with boundless compassion
and be a witness to the reality
of love's continual eruption into the world.

FOR GLIMPSES OF HEAVEN HERE AND NOW

Sacred Source of Joy,
help us to see glimpses
of heaven all around us,
in the urgency of each spring's blooming,
in the simple gifts of water
to bathe in and drink,
in our morning tea or coffee,
with steam rising like this prayer,
in the dog's pleading eyes
or the warm embrace of a friend,
in the food that nourishes us
and the herbs given freely for healing.

May we behold wonder in the way
sunlight illumines and moonlight glows.
May we treasure moments of laughter
and see paradise shimmering forth
wherever we look.
Help us savor moments
of ease and hope in whatever forms they take.
Strengthen and nourish us
to share a vision of Eden with the world.

WHEN THE CALENDAR IS FULL

Holy Keeper of Rhythms,
sometimes I am ruled by my calendar,
its boxes much too full,
every minute accounted for and squeezed.
Bless these appointments
for work, health care, family, friendship,
and all the other details of daily life.

May I be as present as possible
to each person I encounter.
May I shower kindness
even when tired or impatient.

May I find spaces in between
to slow down, to breathe,
to tend my own tender heart,
to listen for your sacred whispers
amid the ordinary.

May I take moments
to watch the sun's rising or setting,
to stand in awe at the moon,
to listen to rain beating the windows,
for Sabbath rest,
and for the holy seasons
of grieving and celebration.

May all my days
become a doorway
to the sacred mysteries
of cycles and seasons,
a calendar of love's rising.

FOR USING TECHNOLOGY WELL

Blessed Source of Wonder,
it truly is a marvel, technology,
and all it allows me to do—
the connections I make,
the new ideas I discover.

There is a shadow side too:
the way it consumes my attention,
the scale of misinformation and harm,
the frustrations when it stops working.

May I be reminded of the grace at work
every time I write an email or message or search online,
and call to mind the people
on the other end of this connection.
Help me to not take this gift for granted
and guide me in its wise use.
Help me to also step back from screens
and dance in meadows and by streams,
to feel sunlight on my face.

Let me use it with purpose and intention,
and when I feel myself drifting
into endless scrolling,
remind me to turn it off,
quiet my heart, and listen for you.

BLESSINGS FOR HEALTH, HEALING, AND WHOLENESS

FOR HEALTH IN TIMES OF ILLNESS

Healing Presence,
be with me as I struggle with illness
and restore me to vibrant health.

May your divine life
radiate through every cell of my body.
May I find consolation in the horizontal
moments of my convalescence,
the gift of sleep lavishly bestowed.

Grant me moments of ease
where I can restfully enter into full presence
to all that is happening within me
and around me.

May I feel myself held in love
by my community and friends,
and know myself as not alone.

In the moments of pain,
gift me strength to breathe deeply.
In the times of fatigue,
gift me the wisdom to surrender.
In the uncertainty and unknowing
of how things will unfold,
gift me with trust that you hold me close
through it all.

Let this time of intimacy
with my body's vulnerability
bring me closer to you and carry the grace of knowing
the preciousness of my days.

WHEN STARTING A NEW MEDICATION

Great Healer,
bless this new medication.
Minimize my side effects
and let it become a balm for my suffering.

I feel uncertain and unsure of what lies ahead,
but I know I am held in your embrace,
which sustains me through the wilderness of illness.

Bless the scientists who have created this gift
to ease my symptoms.
I am grateful for their loving commitment.

Bless others as they walk
with my same condition through life,
that they experience ease and vitality.

Grant me wellness and strength
to continue giving you love and thanks
for the wonders of this world.

FOR THOSE WITH DEMENTIA

Holy Keeper of Memories,
we know the stories of our lives
are sacred texts, revealing your imprint.

We ask you to bless
those with dementia,
whose threads are slowly unraveling
in the tapestry of their lives.

Give them courage
as they walk into the unknown
and the glimmers of recognition
begin to fade.

Soften the fears of forgetting
and remind them of your love
through kindness and touch,
a nourishing meal,
or the joy of a favorite song.

Lavish healing upon them
that they may know that they are never broken.
Ease the heartache of their family.

Help them to know
you carry our memories
like the treasures they are,
and trust that nothing is ever lost
and everything will be made whole again.

FOR MY INNER CHILD

God of Play and Giggles,
of carefree days and innocence,
bless my inner child and guide me toward
simple, childlike joy.

Life has sometimes felt like a burden—
I have had to take on so much as an adult.
I feel responsible for everyone and everything,
and I am tired and overwhelmed.
The little child I was had to grow up too quickly,
and now I seek healing and reconnection.

May I remember those days
before I knew how harsh the world could be,
before bills and betrayals,
when I used my body as much as my mind.

May I return to those times when I was
lost in the glory of the moment, when I laughed freely
and forgot to worry what others were thinking.
And even if I never knew what it was
to really be a child, help me now reach inward
to nurture and protect that part of myself.

Bless me, Holy One, as I walk toward a new future
where my inner child is loved and nurtured,
and where my adult self can surrender to joy.
Let wonder fill my days and help me look
at the world with innocence again.

FOR LIGHT IN OUR SHADOWS

Holy One who embraces all,
help us to welcome the light and warmth of your truth
into the shadow parts of ourselves:
    the shame, the resentment, the too-bigness,
    the rage and grief,
    the longings for things that seem out of reach,
    all that we resist and reject
    and project onto others.
Remind us that your love is bigger
than everything that feels tender and troubled,
all that we would rather not face.

Bless our vision so that we might discover
what lies hidden in our darkest places.
Grant us courage to seek the truth of our lives
so that we might become
the fullest version of ourselves—
integrated, whole, textured,
and sometimes tangled.

Help us claim the hope
that lead can be transformed into gold;
help us trust that you can turn
our shame into dancing.

FOR NEW LIFE

O God of Newness,
infuse me with your greening vitality.

Blessed are those who are weary,
stretched thin, burned out, exhausted,
and blessed are all the ways our bodies
ask for loving care through our symptoms
of pain, fatigue, and dis-ease.

Sustain us in moments
when we feel we can't hold on any longer.
Prepare a resting place for each of us,
a bed of renewing soil.

Plant us deep beneath the rich, dark earth,
for a season of regeneration
until our green tendrils emerge again.

TO EMBRACE QUEERNESS

Holy One of Rainbows and Diversity,
you created violet and cobalt, forest and lime,
sunshine and marigold, rose and crimson,
all vibrant threads in a glorious tapestry.

Help us to embrace
every expression of living
in alignment with your desires for a world
of care and wonder.

Bless us with curiosity and humility
so that we might view living on the edges as gift,
and the unexpected
as a source of grace and creative vision.
Open the doors of our hearts
so that we might extend a lavish welcome
to all that feels strange
or what we do not understand,
and to know these encounters as places
of our breaking open and transformation.

Empower us to always stand
on the side of love—
to reject hate without hesitation,
especially when summoned
in your name.

Let our hearts welcome queerness:
help us to see from new perspectives,
to venture to wild edges,
to have the courage

to be our full and magnificent selves
living out the divine dance with you.

FOR A JOURNEY THROUGH DARK TIMES

Holy One who is ever-present,
even in our darkest nights
and descents to despair,
bless us with a sense of your abiding nearness
as life strips away all our comforts
and securities, everything we thought we needed.

Help us to build our endurance
and strengthen our vision
to see you shimmering in the night.

It is so hard to stay here.
We want to run to brighter fields,
to numb ourselves to the anguish.
Bless us even in this running and numbing,
and guide us back to your presence,
and to the call of this journey,
which is to move through,
to let it break our hearts,
to release all of our old sacred images
so that we might embrace a more expansive
sense of the holy mystery of you, our Source.

Let the wisdom of Mary,
whose own heart was broken open,
be our guide.
Let transformation be our hope—
help us to gently release
our sense of being victim
and embrace our sovereignty
so that our darkest nights

can one day become
luminous with grace for others.

TO EMBRACE THE BELOVEDNESS OF BEING

Holy One, inspire the eyes of our hearts
to see ourselves as beloved just as we are.
Help us remember
there is nothing we need to *do*
to be worthy or loved,
that everything magical and alive
in this stunning world
pulses within us as well.

Each of us is blessed
by the simple fact of being created by you,
our belovedness as close as our own breath.
As your children—
ordinary, weird, and quirky—
we are precious in your sight.

By the fact of our existence,
we have a share in your being
alongside mineral and mountain,
river and flow, the tide ebbing and rising.
The fire of constellations burns within us
as does the breath of your inspiration.

Infuse our dreams with visions
of a world where everyone is loved
just as we are, the tender and trembling parts
welcome alongside the bold and bewitching ones.

Your voice echoes across generations:
I am who am,
and we stand in that presence too,

knowing ourselves as creatures destined for holiness,
flesh redeemed with all our scars and wounds,
the broken places shimmering with your grace.

Bless the circles we stand in,
that we might be seen for who we are
and see others in the light of your love,
each of us a sliver of starlight,
our radiance ringing out across
a galaxy of hope.

FOR FORGIVENESS

Source of Love,
my heart is hurting and I feel betrayed;
my stomach is tangled, my throat burning.
I feel like something was stolen from me,
an abiding trust in others and in the world.

Sit with me in the ache
of grief and anger,
of all the ways I have been wounded.

Bless me with grace and ease;
soften that which has become hard and calcified.
Shower me with gentleness.

I am not ready to forgive—
the hurt still sears,
my tears still rise.

When the pain overcomes me,
guide me to know when to let go enough
so that I don't keep wounding myself.

Help me to know
when forgiveness might be possible,
not as a denial of my pain,
but as a portal to a place
where I can allow that pain to exist
without swallowing me whole.

Let the way be opened
in the right time and season
for healing to fill the cracks

like a balm, like a fountain
overflowing with love.

FOR SUPPORT IN DEPRESSION

Consoling Spirit,
my heart is feeling so very dark.
My mood is flat, my energy is gone.
Sit with me in my depression;
help me not to feel so alone with it all.

The world is such a challenging place to be,
and I am swimming through mud.
Sometimes it is hard to breathe,
and my stomach is in knots.
You know that we all have low tides,
and you won't rush me into a place of light,
but instead promise to abide with me in love.

Bless me with your gentle invigoration.
Give me courage to seek the support I need:
a walk to feel the wind and hear birdsong,
calling a friend who can sit with me in silence,
seeking medication if needed,
creating art to bring this stuckness
into conversation with possibility.

Sustain me through this season,
as long as it takes,
and help my vision to expand
to see all the ways you companion me.

FOR CAREGIVERS

May the Great Sustainer
shower you with care.
May you know yourself
as not just caregiver but also one who receives—
may you drink freely from an overflowing well
and eat your fill at a banquet laid out with lush fruits.
May you find a place to rest for a while.

Blessed are you who care for others,
for you have a heart for connection
and know the power of kindness.
You have felt the humbling need
of dependence on another,
the tenderness in having to ask for help.
Sometimes it can feel like a lot;
there is no real rest
with someone depending on you.
Your heart is full of love,
but you are also tired.

Close your eyes, dear one,
for just a minute,
and feel yourself held,
nourished, revived,
by the One who is the Source of Love
you bestow on others.

See yourself as woven into a tapestry of care,
blessed and sent forth
to help build a gentler world.

FOR REST IN BURNOUT

God, I feel utterly depleted,
unable to summon energy
to do anything anymore.
I have given all my fire to life
and now await its rekindling.

My body needs rest—
    tired and achy, my energy is drained away.
My heart needs rest—
    tender and broken, my compassion feels gone.
My spirit needs rest—
    doubting and unsure, my purpose has vanished.

Great Healer,
pour forth your oil of anointing
and remind me of my wholeness.
Make a resting place for the whole of me.
Even if I am unable to take rest,
lavish it upon me in the cracks of life.

Bless me with assurance
that it isn't all up to me.
Help me to know you are nestled in beside me,
carrying all I can't hold right now,
your tender hand on my brow.

Give me ease so that I can slowly rebuild.
Help me to say no more often
and to claim it as a sacred word—
as holy as any yes.

FOR HEALING A DIVIDED FAMILY

Giver of Life,
my family is divided,
and my heart is broken.
I know there are so many reasons for relationships to rupture:
    betrayal, addiction, violence,
    a slow growing apart,
    a misunderstanding amplified,
    ancestral wounds carried forward.

I long for a sense of connection
to those I am bound to by blood and bone.
I reach out and my advances are rejected,
and it has become painful to reach anymore.

Bless me in this ache and longing.
Help to ease my sorrow
and sense of loss.
Guide me to the next steps
that might open the way forward.
Surround me with friends
who help me know I belong.

May all my efforts at healing
ripple through our family system,
bringing new ways of relating—
if not now, then in generations to come.

FOR BECOMING WISE AND WELL

God of Ancient Vision,
we dream the dreams of old,
the longings of our ancestors
arising in the surrender of the night.

Each choice we make to love,
each moment of kindness,
each speaking of truth
ripples across time.
Each moment that we live into a new way of being
and witness to something different as possible,
we become the world we want to see
and carry forward the desires of the ancients
for peace and ease and joy.

This blessing comes as a call
to release the hold of old compulsions
and what depletes and destroys,
to nourish ourselves with exquisite care,
a reminder that our ancestors ached for us
to bring our ancient birthright of freedom into fullness.

May grandmothers and grandfathers
bless us with clarity and alignment
to bring our gifts in service
to a torn and trembling world.
To do these things with intention
is to elevate their memory with honor.

This blessing comes as a dedication
for love to disrupt all the wounded patterns,

for us to remember where we came from,
but to also commit to the place we are,
here where we know the names of trees and stones,
of flowers and birdsong.

May we be loving guardians of the land beneath our feet.
May our home become a bearer of stories
to leave for the future waiting to be born.

PILGRIMAGE BLESSINGS

FOR SAYING YES TO THE JOURNEY

Holy Traveler,
bless our sacred yes to the call
you have whispered to us,
whether a call to new adventure
or the call that arises out of loss.
We know you journey with us
and guide us on the way to new paths.

May we travel with intentionality,
being conscious of encountering you in each step,
in each stranger, in each moment of disorientation.

We ask you to bless our feet,
    that they carry us forward to new possibilities.
Bless our hands,
    that they might help us give form to our creative visions.
Bless our hearts,
    that we stay open to wonder and numinous moments.
Bless our throats,
    that we gain courage to speak truth.
Bless our lips,
    that we take in what is most nourishing.
Bless our intuition,
    that through wisdom and dreams
    you may be a close companion on the way,
    guiding us through the darkness.

FOR TRAVELING LIGHTLY

Winnowing God,
you ask us to release, let go,
surrender, and yield all that we can
in service of making space for what is most essential.

The more we set aside
that which burdens us and takes up too much space,
the more room opens within us
for wonder and gratitude to flourish,
and the more we find the freedom
to see the world as enchanted.

Sustain us on the path of simplifying our lives
and traveling on this Earth more lightly
so that we no longer live beyond what can be sustained.

As we continue on the pilgrim's path
unencumbered by so many things,
may you open our hearts
to delight in the simple beauty of the world.

FOR GUIDANCE ON OUR WAY

Journeying One,
you help us to navigate the path
and place one foot in front of the other,
even when the way ahead is not visible.

We set aside our desire for maps, GPS, and guidebooks
and surrender to an inner knowing and direction
sparked by the deepest longings of our hearts.
We know our desire for new life
has been kindled by you.

May we surrender our need to steer the course.
With every step we take,
carry us into greater intimacy with you.

Help us to see others as fellow pilgrims on the way
with their own fears and struggles.
Compel us to reach out a hand
in loving compassion and support.
May we recognize all those holy guides
who disrupt our intended paths
as sparking a new direction on our way.

FOR BEGINNING AGAIN

Spirit of Renewal,
as we breathe the fresh morning air,
allow us to see all the places where newness
is being born into the world:
the bud of a flower just breaking open its petals,
the turning of the sea's tides,
a gaze into the eyes of another
to behold their beauty,
the river stone being rubbed smooth.

Help us to remember
that we are always being called to begin again.
Like the prodigal one returning home
to a loving parent's embrace,
relieve our shame or heartache
at wandering so far from you
and reveal to us the feast
you prepare where tables are piled high
with the sweetest of fruits.

FOR STEPPING INTO THE UNKNOWN

God of Wild Edges and New Horizons,
we seek your presence in those moments
when we feel out of place and miss the comforts of home.

Sustain our journey when we feel the ache of strangeness,
the quiver of anxiety, the fear of doubt,
and help us discover a deeper knowing in the midst of it all
that doesn't rely on us desperately clinging to our plans
but calls us to open to the discoveries
arriving on the doorstep within.

Help us hear your nearness in the beating of our hearts
and to hold with courage and trust the paradoxes of life:
communion and loss, beauty and suffering, love and violence,
as invitations into songs of both lament and praise.

Let us be undone by the mystery
of it all, and then refashion us
into wiser, humbler,
and more compassionate wholeness.

FOR COMING HOME

God of Homecomings,
our lives are a pilgrimage journey,
seeking the discovery of home in the world.
We travel not in straight lines
but in circles and spirals, revisiting old patterns
and ways of being that need healing.
Help us trust in life's unfinished nature,
and also the deep desires of our heart,
calling us to reorient ourselves again and again.

Magnify our vision
so that each journey we make leads
to expanded growth and wisdom.

Help us continue to dive into
the refreshing river of life,
allowing the current to carry us closer to you.

Carve out in us a space for both grief and joy
so that we may meet life with eyes and hearts wide open.

Remind us of the ancient pilgrims who travel with us unseen,
and guide us beyond boundaries to experience you,
drawing us closer to our own wild edges.

In those moments when we do arrive home,
give us the deep rest we desire,
where we remember your presence in all that we do.

BLESSINGS FOR OUR CONNECTION TO THE HOLY WILD

FOR KINSHIP WITH CREATION

God of Lavish Fecundity,
you overflow into nature in every moment,
offering your gifts of beauty and nourishment.

Nurture me with sacred rhythms of light and dark,
rising and falling, fullness and emptiness,
as the pulse of your loving presence
animates every living thing.

Help me to remember my own wildness
so that I come to know
every bird, fish, insect,
and animal as kin
and to live in ways that renew and sustain
Earth and all her systems.

Renew my vision so that I see
beyond the barriers I have constructed.

Kindle my longing to join the great song
of the sea, the trees, the mountains, and the flowers,
which are already singing your praise,
and to live as a member of the great community of creation.

FOR THE EARTH, OUR SANCTUARY

God of All That Is Green and Wild,
help us to find sanctuary among trees and stones,
and feel Earth preparing a place for us
to sit and breathe and be.

As the long limbs of branches
form a canopy above our heads,
let the hills open up a place for our spirits to soar.
The stones serve as your altars,
and the sun makes everything shimmer and glisten;
all of creation shines forth from within.
Let the tender vine climbing the trunk
show us what it is to reach to the sky;
let all the living creatures that gather here,
winged and four-footed ones,
offer us a sign of your companionship.

You have made us part of this glorious cathedral—
the lakes and holy wells are fonts of new life,
the river rushes to carry gifts down from the mountains,
the oaks and sycamores reach out
to draw us into their sacred circle,
which reveals your face, Creator of us all,
incarnate and immanent
and illuminated by the natural wonder of all we gaze upon.

May the veil between heaven and earth slip away
so that we may more intimately know
this sanctuary of soil and sunlight;
may we listen to the sky whisper her secrets on the wind,
and be lifted by wings and song.

FOR OUR JOURNEY THROUGH THE SEASONS

Creator of All,
open our eyes to your Word
scribed on every leaf and petal,
on every wing and paw.

As the seasons unfold in their vibrant dance of change,
may we read on their pages your call
to blossom forth, to bear fruit,
to surrender and yield, to rest into mystery.

Let the journey of caterpillar to moth
teach us the path of transformation.
Let the patience of mountains and the singing of stones
give us guidance for what it means to endure.
Let the rise and fall of the sun and moon
circling the blue-tiled sky
teach us about journeys to fullness
and to rest and release.

May your Holy Wisdom be revealed in each season,
that we might recognize grace at every turn.

TO HEAR OUR CALLING THROUGH CREATION

Holy One,
bless us with the wisdom
to live fully as the people you created us to be,
with no doubt or hesitation.
Help us to become people
who know our sacred purpose like
an oak tree possesses majesty,
an owl owns the night,
a stream quietly sings,
and marigolds lift their faces with joy.

May the fireflies light our way in the darkness,
may the morning glory spark gratitude for a new day,
may the witness of feather and hoof,
leaf and light, reveal to us what it means to be
truly, wholly, fully ourselves.
Break open the sacred seed of your Spirit
planted deep within us.

May we cherish the badger who ambles across the Earth,
the raven painting the sky,
the horse galloping over the meadow,
and note how they spark our own longing
to run or fly into your arms,
you who know our name,
the One who has always been etched in our hearts
from the very first moment.

FOR LEARNING FROM THE WISDOM OF NATURE

Sacred Source of All,
bless us with vision so that we might see
that everything in creation can become
a catalyst for more deeply understanding ourselves.

Let the sacred whispers carried on the wind
invite us to release what is not necessary.
Let the breezes help our spirits to ascend,
and may the sparrows remind us of our own flock.
Let your divine fire, which burns in our hearts,
kindle us to deeper compassion.
Grant us your sunlight to seek illumination.

Let the rivers and seas support us in allowing
your Spirit to flow through our lives in new ways,
and embracing the rise and fall of what our days bring us.
Let the pine cones contain an epiphany,
and each smooth stone, a revelation.
May the forest invite us to embrace your truth once again.

Let the moon sing to us of quiet miracles,
like those that reveal and conceal the world every day
right before our eyes.

May we make time to listen to the elements
in their wisdom, revealing your holy face
and the sacred direction for our one precious life.

A LAMENT FOR CREATION

Beloved, we gaze upon creation
as a holy icon revealing the face of your love.

We see the beauty of this green Earth
and feel the ache of our neglect,
the exploits, the ravages, the scars we have left
across field and mountain.
We welcome a river of tears
for all that suffers,
and do not resist the grief of beholding
    the otter choked with oil,
    the sky darkened with grime,
    the seas heavy with plastic,
    the koalas fleeing the great fire.

We make room for a world of sorrow,
we make the Earth's anguish our song,
and we allow grief to bloom and grow.

We ask you, the Source of Love who created our tears
and tender hearts, and with them
the promise of reconciliation,
to create a new place within,
where a different story can arise,
where we can all turn toward a vision
of wholeness once again.

FOR SAVORING THE WILD SACRAMENT OF CREATION

May Christ who shimmers in all creation
surprise you each day with glittering moments,
that you can see again
how light lives in everything:
how it partners
with dark soil to bring forth
aster and lavender,
rosemary and daffodils,
a hundred kinds of squash,
kale and cabbage, apple and berry,
grapes sweetened by the sun.

May the Creator reveal
how the dough you knead in your hands
is an alchemy of touch and time;
how everything is
a call to communion—
the wafer of moon,
a chalice of stars.

Let the mystery of it all
dance in your heart,
always widening your horizons,
that you may inhabit new landscapes.

May you know each moment as sacred
and everything around you a call
to remember this one true thing.

A SONG OF PRAISE

Singer of the Cosmic Song,
bless us with ears
to listen to how everything sings:
streams and stones,
leaves and branches,
fish and fur-covered ones,
with birds leading the chorus.

Help us to see how your joy and generosity
are echoed in every living thing;
how in quiet moments
the heart is moved to gratitude
for all of creation,
for the lavish abundance of it all;
how nothing is earned
and no achievements are needed.

May we simply show up
with breath, blood, and bones,
and offer loving attention to hymns erupting
everywhere, until we can no longer tell
where our song begins and nature's ends.

TO BE BLESSED BY THE GIFTS OF THE ELEMENTS

God of the Wild Elements,
bless us through your gifts of wind, fire, water, and earth.
May we awaken to new life each dawn
and feel your holy breath sustaining us.

May the breezes whisper their secrets
and the winds strip away what is no longer needed.
May we bless the sky with our reaching,
the clouds a witness to our becoming.
May we feel the living flame of love
burning in our hearts.

May the sun warm and illumine us,
and may the ash that remains
from the fire bring us new clarity.
May we bless the fire with our passion,
letting all that sparks and blazes within us
warm this world.

May we know the sea as our holy source,
and may the rivers and lakes carry us
on currents of love.
Let the holy water of the wells
heal our broken places,
bringing us back to wholeness again.
May we bless the water of life
and yield to its flow as it carries us home.

May we bless Earth with our gratitude,
for the sweetness of every sip and bite.

Let the trees root us; let the mountains lift us.
May we endure like stone;
may we nourish like bread.
May the elements guide us on the way
to live more fully, to breathe deeply,
to ignite our longings, to follow the flow,
to create something that persists.

BLESSINGS FOR THE SEASONS

DURING ADVENT

God of Holy Birthing,
journey with us this Advent season
as we too say yes to new dreams, gestate new visions,
and bring to life new radiance in the world.

Blessed is this season of humble beginnings
and the promises of luminous grace
set to burst forth like juice from the ripest plum.
We witness Mary as she partners with the divine
to make your Word incarnate.
We wait with her to see the shape of things to come.

We walk into the darkest of nights
with only the stars for guidance,
and the ancient story as a companion.
We feel the ground tremble at the significance
    of this yes we remember year after year,
    of justice singing a new song,
    of the magic and goodness of every living being,
    of a deep breath of liberation for all creation,
    of sweetness erupting into every corner of bitterness.

Sustain us as we wait and stumble,
as we sit with doubt and unknowing,
until the moment when the Holy Child
opens our eyes in wonder
to behold a world worth loving
with a heart as wide as the cosmos.

TO EMBRACE HOLY DARKNESS

God of Mystery,
you grace Earth with seasons
and call your creation into rhythms
of flowering and fruitfulness,
release and rest.

Help us surrender to winter's invitation
to slow down, to listen, to lie fallow, to be.
Abide with us in the holy darkness,
as our certainties and securities come undone
and the stars pulse across the night sky.

Sustain us as we gestate new possibilities,
hidden and unseen to us, like tiny seeds
preparing to flourish into fullness.
Embrace us as we rest our bodies, hearts,
minds, and spirits, and discover again
the goodness of sleep, dreaming, and slowness.
Reveal to us how letting go of our need for answers
allows us to ponder beautiful questions.

Bless this season of the dark
so that we might be transformed and renewed,
ready when spring comes
to bring to birth your love
and to shower it generously everywhere we go.

TO FOLLOW MARY AS GOD-BEARER

Mary, you were called
to become a bearer of God,
to carry the weight and lightness
of heaven and earth joined
together in the Holy Child.
Blessed is your yes,
sacred is your womb,
divine is its fruit.

Be with us as we too
are called to be God-bearers.
Bless us as we birth the holy
into the world,
as we carry the weight
of our callings and gifts,
as we feel both the gravity of their heaviness
and take flight with their lightness.

May we know ourselves
as flesh infused with spirit's radiance.
Mary, come be a midwife for our wild dreaming.
Support us as we birth a new promise into the world.

Help us to breathe through our labor,
to feel the quickening of our hearts as we bring
to fruition all that has been growing inside of us.

Place this creation into our arms
so that we might behold the fruit
God has brought to fullness in us.

ON WINTER SOLSTICE

Holy One who turns the earth,
we watch the daily pilgrimage of the sun
as its journey grows shorter and shorter.

Bears, bats, and hedgehogs rest
while swallows and swifts have
already migrated south again.

Cold air, bare branches, blankets, and shawls—
the growing quiet calls us to our own retreat.
Then a bell rings out across the hemisphere;
the diminishment pauses,
then slowly shifts back toward the light.
We imagine our ancestors standing
in the heart of winter's cold darkness
with faces upward in awe each year
as your brilliance begins
to brighten the sky more and more each day,
gold beams tumbling like treasure.

We know on this day the light will grow again,
a tiny seed at first, then a shy blooming.
Help us to see our own inner seasons
of darkness and light as necessary gifts
of rest and illumination.
May we become this light for others,
and bear the promise of radiance emerging
from every place that feels cold and dark.

ON CHRISTMAS

Incarnate One,
we dance at the doorway
of light and dark as the seasons change,
and know both as sacred,
for you chose the fertile space of a womb
to join us in the miracle of birth.

Come to us now,
that we might participate in those moments of labor
that birth the holy
into this fragile, luminous, hurting world

as Mary did two thousand years ago,
eyes wide, hands gripping,
waters breaking like crashing waves
of the primordial sea,
sending a prayer through time
that echoes still,
pulsing like starlight
in an enormous sky.

Come to us now that we might also rest a hand
on the back of the lonely
  disoriented
    lost
      hungry
        despairing
          persecuted.
Remind us that our humanity is not an obstacle
but a threshold;
remind us that the wound is a portal

through which your gifts pour forth,
that the raw ache we feel
is the terrible wonder of being alive
calling us into a communion
of veil-lifters who catch glimpses
of a world where the greeds
and horrors are turned upside down.

Come to us now with an Annunciation:
the world needs us to be wild edge-dwellers,
where the wind cries out,
where the stone endures,

our hands a bowl,
our hearts a cave,
our eyes a mirror,
to bring a drink of water,
an ancient song,
a shimmering light,
and reflect all that we miss
in days of rushing.

Come to us now and create a resting place
where we can gather strength
from your presence here within,
between the diastole and systole
of our very hearts,
and learn to trust your nearness
in roses and pomegranate,
in sparrows and dragonflies,
in the electricity of the storm.

Come to us now that we might know
your birthing among us

is not once and for all
but again and again,
erupting like moonlight
between bare branches,
like a hearth fire lit
for all who have been exiled.
Come to us now and call us home.

FOR THE NEW YEAR

We call on the Holy One of Newness,
who reveals all that is fresh and alive and wondrous,
to bless us as we cross this threshold
into a new beginning.

Bless us with a word of wisdom
that glimmers and guides the way into the year ahead.
In moments of uncertainty, let your Word be an anchor;
in times of grief, let your Word carve out space in us
to lament and weep;
in times of celebration, let your Word confirm
all that is good and beautiful in our lives.
Let your Word call us back always to love,
echoing our heart's deepest desires.

Let your Word weave its way
through all the holy ordinary moments
so that we might remember our wholeness
and respond with generosity to a world in need.

We ask for your blessing
that we might become a blessing to others
in the year ahead.

ON EPIPHANY

Luminous One,
help us to see the world with new eyes.
Open our hearts to behold the star
that directs us to our true call.
Allow us to see all that glistens around us
and inspire us to a grateful heart.
Reveal to us the places that need
our compassion and our lavish care.
Support us in bringing deep peace into the world
through our words and actions.
Help us to see more clearly
all the ways we can embody your love in the world.

Like the Wise Ones,
let us bring our gifts in service
of cultivating *shalom* in our midst.

Strengthen us to welcome your holy surprises,
break through into our night-dreams,
and guide us on a new pathway
home again.

ON IMBOLC AND THE FEAST OF ST. BRIGID

Imbolc is a traditional Celtic festival to mark the start of spring on the feast of St. Brigid, February 1.

Spirit of Rebirth,
your new life pulses below the rumbling ground.
Attune our ears
to the renewal taking form
beneath the winter earth,
snowdrops and crocuses
in white and purple-petaled wonder,
hedgehogs and bears
beginning to stir from sleep.

Let Brigid be our guide
as we navigate the way
from rest to slow emergence;
support us in nourishing
the fragile seeds of possibility.

May her birds, the oystercatchers,
    lift our hearts on currents of love.
May her devoted cow
    remind us of generous abundance.
May the perpetual flame of her purpose
    kindle our own sparks of initiative.
May her mantle embrace us
    and offer protection.
May the waters of her sacred wells
    bless and refresh us
    for the journey ahead.

As the bellies of ewes
are filling with new life
across the green meadows,
may we remember to cherish
the new birth getting ready to erupt
all around and within us.

If the landscape around us
looks bleak, help us trust
a deeper knowing,
a promise of what is to come.

ON ASH WEDNESDAY

God of New Beginnings,
bless these ashes as markers of our mortality,
calling us to cherish this one radiant life
and to commit to presence, holiness, compassion,
creativity, slowness, and wonder.

Let these ashes become signs
of how much we love this world
and how we are called to live in new ways,
counter to the relentless productivity
and violence of our times.

Baptize us anew, God of Refreshment;
clear a path to our hearts.
Help us remember our divine inheritance
so that we may rise up, empowered by your love,
to welcome the stranger,
to bring mercy and kindness to a hurting world,
to find you in each moment and encounter.

Let this Ash Wednesday become the time
we remember as when we stepped fully
into our truest selves, reflections of you.

FOR A LENTEN JOURNEY

Holy One of the Desert and Wilderness,
you have called our hearts to follow you
into places that strip away
all that is not essential
and to rest in your abiding love.

Meet us on the dry, shifting sand
or the wild thicket where we have wandered out
to find ourselves and you.
Walk with us as we do the hard inner work
to stay present to you even amid
the difficult voices, the challenging thoughts,
the harsh judgments.

Celebrate with us those moments on our journey
when there is a clearing,
moments when stillness
rises like a mountain,
moments when we know what it is to simply be.

Illuminate our vision to see all that we grasp
and cling to, all that burdens us,
all that makes us feel divided.

Let the dross burn in the holy fire,
until we see your radiance
shimmering at every turn,
in each face, in each encounter.

Help us to see how much in love
with the world you are,
how you beckon us to follow.

ON THE SPRING EQUINOX

God of Balance,
we ask your blessing at this threshold
when light and dark are equal.

Teach us to welcome both
into our lives, to make room for joy and sorrow,
for sunlight's shimmering and moonlight's radiance.

As the light continues to grow
and birds and insects begin their migrations,
journeying by impulse and intuition,
help us listen to your call
to move in a holy direction.

Inspire us to celebrate the burgeoning
and blossoming of buds
all around us as well as within our hearts.

Holy Gardener, sustain us in nourishing
this season of growth,
cultivate trust in us that we are blooming
something the world needs.

Let the wondrous colors of creation
remind us of the grace in diversity.
Ignite our spirits and our feet
to enter into this sacred dance
of awakening with you.

ON THE FEAST OF THE ANNUNCIATION

Mary, Blessed Virgin,
we give thanks for your strength and power,
for your clarity of purpose,
for your alignment of vision with the divine imagination.

Bless us with a heart that knows the treasure we are;
let our yes rise up like a sacred song we know by heart.
Blessed are you, complete unto yourself;
you are in touch with the promise
of wholeness we each contain.
When the angel asked his question,
everything in you trembled.
You knew the weight of this choice
and could see that moment rippling out into the world.
So you breathed into your fullness, felt the weight and density
of your own presence, and said that holy, mighty, potent yes.

Mary, be with us in our own moments of annunciation.
When the angel whispers to us in a dream,
or shimmers forth in our lives, help us to listen closely,
to slow down and know this moment for the gift it is.

Help us remember our own sanctity and wholeness,
to respond not from any sense of lack
but from an abundance of grace flowing
freely within us all the time, at every moment.

Bless us in our own virginity,
to know the gift we bring
into the world as wholly ours to offer.

Let this moment be an invitation
into a deeper intimacy
with the divine presence dwelling in our hearts.
Help us to say yes.

DURING HOLY WEEK

God of Truth and Paradox,
in these coming days
you call us to sit in the heart of betrayal, abandonment,
mockery, violence—
to not avert our eyes
but see ourselves in the story.

Travel with us into
the border spaces of unknowing
and hold us as we behold both death and life
in the liminal realm of in-between.

As we feel the suffering and loss of Jesus,
let us not rush to resurrection just yet,
but linger a while in mystery.
In this temple of grief,
strip us of our attachments,
the identities we cling to,
the securities we believe in.
Disorient us
so that we might walk in a new direction.
Lift the veils
that dull our senses from the world's sorrow.
Give us courage
to ask questions rather than seek answers.
Let loss carve a space within us to let love pour
into this chalice of the heart.

Bring us into communion
with all those who suffer
from poverty, hunger, war, abuse,

climate crises, pollution, clear-cutting—
the whole of creation groaning
together in labor.
Help us to birth a new possibility,
one only dimly seen
in quiet moments
and arise as a glimmer in the eyes
or a song in the throat.

ON EASTER

God of Rising,
you bring new life
to all the places death inhabits.

Bless our own dying dreams
with your breath of new life.
Make our dry bones dance,
inspire us to sing,
revive our bodies
so that we might become
more vibrant, hopeful witnesses
to the persistence of your love.

We call on Christ's wisdom
to bless and sustain us
in the practice of resurrection
by which we honor our bodies
and become agents of generous abundance.

May all the nets we draw up from the water
be overflowing with fish,
may our wounds be still visible
as a sign of healing grace,
and may we encounter your presence
when we sit at table with strangers.

Let our lives be a celebration
of all the ways your love thrives
where once there was only doubt,
like the first riot of daffodils in spring.

ON BELTANE AND THE START OF SUMMER

Beltane is a Celtic feast that celebrates the beginning of summer on May 1—it marks the half of the year that is filled with light.

Holy One of Lavish Generosity,
infuse us with gratitude for all you create.
Bless us with fertility at any stage of life.
If our hearts feel dry and dusty,
shower us with your life-giving dew.

The season of the fertile earth begins,
reminding us in color and scent
and juicy offerings of sweetness
how we too are called
to this eruption of creativity.

Make us like Mary, that we might birth the holy.
Make us like Jesus, that we might build a vision
of abundance for all beings.

Let us know the goodness and pleasure
of it all as part of your holy desire.
Let us overflow with the gladness of tangerines
and the joy of peonies, gathering all beings
into our circle of celebration.

ON PENTECOST

Spirit of Courage,
we stand huddled too,
like the disciples in the upper room,
wondering what is real and true anymore.

Reveal to us the pulse of your fire
in each of our hearts
and send us with bread and roses
out into a world
hungry for nourishment.

Bless us with visions of peace;
carry it across every sky
on wings of a dove.
Help us understand one another
so that we might know
our common purpose in love.

Let the winds of change
rush in and upend all our fears.
Empower us for a more
just and loving future
where we dance with your wild grace.

ON THE SUMMER SOLSTICE

Radiant One,
creator of the cosmos
and the heavenly luminaries that light our way,
bless this day of longest light
and the gift of the sun,
which brings warmth to our lives
and abundance of growth,
the sweetness of blueberries,
the refreshment of lemons,
the nourishment of kale
and a thousand other kinds of food.

We sing in gratitude
along with the sparrows and robins
that arise each morning
to celebrate another day.

Help us remember
the universe came into being
fourteen billion years ago
with ancient skies unfurling,
stars spilling across the heavens
and manifesting in every living thing.

Your light is our inheritance
and calls us to be bearers of radiance.
Bring forth new life in us
from the fertile darkness.

ON LUGHNASA AND THE START OF THE HARVEST SEASON

Lughnasa is a Celtic feast that celebrates
the start of the harvest season on August 1.

Spirit of the Harvest,
help us gather in the goodness
of all we have sown these last few months.

From the seeds of food we have planted
to the dreams we have cultivated,
bless all that has come to fullness
so that it be in service of life.

Fill our baskets with sweet fruits
and plentiful grain to nourish us
for the months ahead.

Let blackberries stain our fingers
and staffs of wheat be transformed
into bread to share with others.

Spark gratitude in our hearts
for this moment of fullness
so that we know ourselves as vessels of your abundance.

As the sun's arc across the sky begins to lower,
and the air hints at autumn's crispness,
usher us into a new season of life,
one filled with kindness and care
for everyone who struggles.

Let this harvest be a gathering in of love.

ON THE FEAST OF THE TRANSFIGURATION

Radiant God,
bless us with vision
and open our eyes to all the ways
the sacred shimmers before us:
    how gold pours forth from the robin's throat,
    how sunlight returns each morning,
    how the moon glitters across still water,
    how laughter around the table kindles joy,
    how kindness can change lives.

Free us from our need to seize these moments,
to make of them stone monuments
rather than tabernacles of light
we carry with us in our hearts.

This vision is a call
not to stay on the mountain
but to gather our treasures
into an open embrace,
to make the slow pilgrimage into the world,
to share them freely after our descent
with a world so hungry for beauty.

Help us to remember
to keep our minds and hearts clear, attuned,
present to your unfolding before us.

Let us see your glow
erupting in all the hidden corners,
in all the places you
have been forgotten.

ON THE FEAST OF THE GUARDIAN ANGELS

Angels of light,
shower us with blessings like a love note
being scrawled across the bright sky.
Gently whisper when we feel stretched thin,
when loneliness swallows us,
when our hearts are unsettled,
or we feel utterly and completely lost.

As we breathe slowly and close our eyes in prayer,
we attune to the warmth of your sheltering wings
and yield to your loving presence.
When prayer feels impossible,
sing the sweetest sounds and
kindle a new song in our hearts.

Lift our spirits, wrap your courage
around us, guide our inner compass
to where we most need to be.
Infuse our souls with the grace of peace.

The span of your wings
weaves together heaven and earth,
on a loom of love.
Help us lift our voices in song
to join with your celestial harmony.

May we pay attention
to shimmering moments
and know you, our guardian angel,
who has beckoned us to pause,
to know this life as gift.

Bring us back
into alignment with the holy desire for God's will
and refresh us with sacred dew.

ON THE FEAST OF ST. FRANCIS OF ASSISI

God of the Wilderness, God of the Dance,
you gave us the example of Francis
to show us what it means to embody love on Earth.

He danced in celebration
of everything you created:
the sun, moon, stars,
water, wind, earth, and fire.
He called them each brother or sister;
he cherished the bird, the wolf, and the grasshopper.
Even death became an intimate companion,
a teacher of how precious life is.

Francis saw the whole world as his monastery,
as the place where your sacred presence
shimmers forth like silver.

Bless us with the courage to follow his example
of holy foolishness, to find our purpose and joy
in a life committed to freedom for all.

Support us to live in alignment with our own sacred purpose
and to remember that when each of us says yes,
transformation is not only possible but inevitable.

ON THE FEAST OF ALL SAINTS

May the communion of saints
shower you with blessings,
and may you seek their guidance
in moments of illness, confusion, gratitude.
We remember their struggle
to enflesh your grace and tenderness.
We ask those across the threshold to pray for us,
for they know what it is to be wounded.

Call on the canonized saints—
Benedict, Francis, Ignatius, Oscar Romero,
Hildegard, Kateri Tekakwitha, Josephine Bakhita—
and the saints of spirit,
such as Howard Thurman, Dorothy Day, Thea Bowman,
and thousands of others
who witnessed to another way of being,
who helped to build a community of love.

Tether us to the earthiness of these men and women,
and remind us of the holiness
they lived with bone and blood.
Give us the grace to use our bodies
to bring love to the world
and reveal the presence of heaven here and now.

Your saints stretch themselves
back across the veil toward us
in sacred friendship,
eyes shining, hearts radiant,
wisdom pouring like rainfall
after months of drought.

They come with a reminder
that we are never alone,
never forsaken.
As we dance in those life-giving showers,
empower us to celebrate your love
as a visible and invisible force
animating the world.

ON THE FEAST OF ALL SOULS

Ancient Wisdom,
you call us to dance with generations
who shimmer beyond the veil.
Reveal to us our shared humanity,
an inheritance we receive in blood and bone.

We call on the great cloud of witnesses
who inspire our courage,
support our endurance,
kindle our joy, whisper words of hope.

May the wise and well ones,
who are vibrant and radiant with healing,
who have stepped into the expanse of love
without hesitation, whose hearts are open wide,
shower us with their blessing
so that we know our ancient inheritance.

We stand at a threshold
and whisper the names
of our grandmothers and grandfathers
back through hundreds and thousands of years,
reaching with our prayers and supplications
for their wisdom and faithfulness
to navigate this world with integrity.
May they form a circle of protection around us
to guard against anything that would wish us harm.

Open the eyes of our hearts to see
they are already here, already dancing
through our feet, our hips, our hands,

the embrace of our arms,
the undulations of our spines,
the smiles on our lips.

May we perceive them dancing
with us in the threshold space
at the turning of dawn or dusk,
helping our hearts stay open and attuned
to the wisdom you pour forth.

We sing our gratitude and ask them to surround us,
knowing they are already present here and now,
ready to help us see our place in a lineage of love.

FOR SOMEONE CELEBRATING A BIRTHDAY

You've made another circle around the sun,
and we ask the Great Sustainer of Breath
to bless you with vitality and vibrancy.
We celebrate the preciousness of these days
and the gifts you bring into a world so hungry for what you offer.

We imagine God's holy delight in you,
which sings through the cosmos
as you reflect on this past year's harvest
and what you long for in the year to come.

As you hold out those dreams with open arms,
we ask for the blessings you seek,
that they may rain down with silver abundance from the sky,
and rise up like greening newness from Earth.

We ask God to weave this silver and green together
into a cord of life that travels
through every vessel of your body,
renewing you and bringing strength for what is to come.

May the Spirit of life quiet your heart
so that you might hear the holy desires
for your time on this beautiful Earth,
and receive them as you would
a gushing fountain on a hot day.

May this birthday mark the crossing of a threshold
that allows you to become even more yourself,
to know love as your purpose,
and to embrace all that you carry forward as grace.

ON THE ANNIVERSARY OF A DEATH

Holy One,
hold me close as I remember
my beloved one, who is gone like dust.
They have passed through the veil
to dwell among the saints and ancestors.

My heart is sick with grief and longing.
Nothing can fill the space of their absence.
Help me to hold open this gap of loss,
to know that it arises from the depth of love.

On this sacred date of remembrance,
I honor the threshold of my own life
and the inevitable loss of those I love.
I celebrate the laughter and delight we shared together,
I bless the vulnerabilities,
I remember any disruptions with compassion,
I cherish the simple moments of sitting together
over tea or a meal, the trips taken, secrets shared,
gifts exchanged, the way we cared for one another in illness,
and the glow of their eyes when I entered the room.

I cherish these ordinary times as sacred,
for they shimmered with the beauty of our humanity.
Bless me in this sanctuary of memory,
and help me to feel their hands reach across the threshold,
to know we are still connected
as if by a golden thread.

THRESHOLD BLESSINGS

FOR A CIRCLE OF COMPANIONS

Great Gatherer,
draw us together in the shelter
of your love and care.
Create among us a communion,
a work of art revealing your heart.
Welcome in all the disparate parts of us
so that we might experience a homecoming.

Bless us with listening,
and deep attunement to one another.
Bless us with shared laughter
and a spark of joy to lighten our hearts.
Bless us with tears
so that we might know ourselves as not alone.
Bless us with rich silences,
a space to rest alongside each other.

May our conversations and presence
awaken us to new possibilities
so that the fruits of our time together
ripple out into the world
as a sign of kinship and loving hospitality.

For the Crossing of a Threshold

Holy One of the Threshold,
you forever reveal to us
new doorways in our lives,
powerful crossing-over places
filled with possibilities.

Give us courage to stay awake and alert
to all the moments when these portals appear.
Inspire us to dance and sing as we wander
into liminal spaces, where the old is stripped away
and the new is waiting to be born.

Be with us as a holy midwife,
and sit with us in the waiting.
Bring us guidance and a sense of your nearness
in the form of signs and symbols—
a stone, a leaf, the song of the river, a night dream—
and infuse us with the wisdom to pay attention.

FOR BOUNTIFUL HOSPITALITY

Holy Presence of God,
you shimmer in every stranger I encounter,
whether in the world or in my heart.

When you came in human form,
you sat at table with all those who walked the edges
of life and honored their presence as sacred.

Create in me a space to welcome in
all that is hard and disorienting.
Help me experience your peace
in those moments when I feel lost, angry,
heartbroken, overwhelmed, ashamed, or sorrowful;
deepen my gratitude when I feel joyful or in love with life.

Help me to honor the guests who arrive at my door,
to usher in the grace that offers newness
and find Christ's compassionate presence there.

May your infinite compassion grow in me
in the way sunlight spills across a field
so that I might include everyone in your loving embrace.

FOR INSPIRATION TO BEGIN AGAIN

God of Holy Surprises,
infuse me with your wild wonder,
attune my heart to all the ways
you dance through the world,
from the ordinary to the sublime.

Sustain me in the daily practice
of opening my eyes to grace.
Expand my imagination to see
more deeply and more widely than before.
Align me with the ways you are constantly at work,
always extending a new vision
when all seems shut down.

Bless my experience of change
as the eruption of seeds in springtime—
plant in me trust in your promise of abundance
and help me grow toward your generous love.

Inspire me to begin again and again.

FOR COMFORT WHEN FACING THE UNKNOWN

Eternal One,
as creator of light and darkness,
you both illuminate and veil.
Be with us in our desire to know,
in our ache to be certain,
in our longing for assurance.

Sit with us in the long, quiet nights
and hold us in our winter seasons.
Wrap us in grace as we confront mystery
and seek your comfort.
Help us rest our thoughts in this mantle of unknowing.

Remind us of how everything emerges
from the dark, fertile womb
of new beginnings, from the black, rich soil of potential
where seeds are planted.

Sustain us in the times when
not knowing is painful, fearful, anguished.

Abide with us in the space
of sacred mystery.
Bring comfort and whisper
words of love to us in the silence.

WHEN IT FEELS AS IF THE WORLD IS ENDING

Holy Ground of Love,
the world so often feels as if it is ending
with news of wars raging, children dying,
fires burning, floods rising—
so much suffering, so much cruelty.

My heart feels like a tree rotting away,
my throat is full of gravel,
my gut a boulder,
my eyes swollen with tears.
With the future tangled with so much loss,
it all feels impossible.

Bless all those who are suffering
because of injustice, loss, and greed.
Ease their pain
and grant them a vision of new life.

Bless me with clarity
to remember that your love is the foundation.
Bless me with guidance
to be a vessel of compassion and peace.
Connect me to kindred souls
laboring for a more beautiful world
so that I know I am not doing this alone.
Turn the hearts of those in power
toward compassion and generosity.

I don't know if what I am called to do will solve anything.
All I know is I must try.
Bless me in the trying, in the grieving, in the hoping.

FOR HOPE IN GRIEF

God of Joy and Sorrow,
you are a midwife to our weeping.
Hold us in our times of grief and loss,
and be with us as we give expression to our love.
Bathe us in the balm of healing.
Gather our tears in the vial of your compassion.
Wash us clean.

When we reach for strength and resist our sorrow,
be a sanctuary for us,
show us where the river of our sobs
meets the great sea of grief.
Let wave upon wave carry us
to the shores of your love.

Remind us we are not alone in our sense of loss,
sanctify our tender places,
make holy our human frailty.

Help us to know
grief and joy as sisters,
to let loss carve us out
to make room for a newfound delight.

FOR WISDOM TO BECOME AN ELDER

Hagia Sophia, Holy Wisdom,
guide us as we harvest our experience and memory.
Help us reflect on how life
has gifted us with meaning.

Let us receive her blessing
as we stand at the threshold of elderhood.
Let it be a warm embrace
and a call to new life.

More than the number of candles on our cake,
growing to maturity is an initiation,
a passage into a new way of being,
one in which we grow more deeply and fully
into the people we were created to be.

Help us find ways to offer ourselves
as a generous presence to others,
listening more than speaking,
witnessing more than seeing,
being more than doing.

Give us prudence and courage
to live in the world you want to create,
to become a breathing sign of your love and peace.

May you be a wild presence for us,
calling us to hold nothing back any longer.

Bless the Earth with your dancing
and the sky with your song.

FOR COURAGE TO BEFRIEND DEATH

Holy Creator,
you formed us from the dust of the earth
by gathering up mud and dirt
in your warm hands, molding and shaping
and sending your spirit through us
until we came alive
and breathed and danced and loved.

These dusty origins began
with stars exploding miles away,
with eons of light expanding and contracting
to arrive in this tender human form.

May we remember
our roots in Earth's rich soil
and heaven's luminous reach.

May we know ourselves
as radically and tenderly embodied
but also radiant with your Spirit,
who sustains our every moment.

May death become a sister
as our friend St. Francis taught—
a wise one to help us see
all that is essential in our lives.

May she help us yield
thoughts, patterns, and ways of being
that distract us and exhaust us,
and empower us to inhabit
the fullness of love's call.

Strip us of regret
so that when our physical end
does finally arrive, we can step across
that bright doorway with arms wide
and hearts open, ready to be gathered
back fully into your embrace.

TO STAY ANCHORED IN THE SACRED

God of Our Pilgrimage Through Life,
I know my future self
will get caught up in plans and busyness,
will worry about bills and climate crisis,
will grieve and ache and rage.

In those moments when my heart sinks,
when I breathe ill at ease,
when my stomach binds in knots,
remind me to

pause,

breathe deeply,
then again,
and a third time.
As I make the slow pilgrimage from head to heart,
let your presence descend into my body.

Rest there in my inner cave,
a sanctuary and dwelling place for you, my Beloved,
who is shimmering, whispering, twirling with delight.

Help me remember my journey, each tender footstep,
each new awakening and insight.
Send your angels
for protection, guidance, wisdom, and healing.
I ask all the saints to pray for a shower of blessings
and invite the ancestors who dreamed me into being
to dance in a circle around me
and flood me with love and golden light.

Keep me in the knowledge that they never left,
that it was only my vision that was distorted
in the world's rush and frenzy
when I lost my way for a moment.

Help me hear them singing, "Return to us again and again,"
and remember the way home,
following it like the pulse of my blood,
like a pathway circling the heart.

FOR PATIENCE IN WAITING

Holy One, abide with us
in the challenging space of waiting.
We wait for news,
for notifications, for changes,
and this dim corridor can feel lonely.

Surround us with kindred souls
who rest beside us in unknowing
and leave behind easy advice.

Spirit, breathe through us,
hold us steady.
Let our inhale and exhale
become an anchor in uncertainty.

Bless us with patience
to take each moment as it comes,
to spend the long hours
calling on you for consolation,
to know that whatever the outcome,
love is a balm for all wounds,
a lever for what we cannot bear.

Source of Newness,
rest quietly here with us.
Behold our heart's longings,
enfold us in your solace,
and when the waiting finally ends,
shower us with the wisdom we need
to walk gently into our unfolding future.

BEFORE GOING ON RETREAT

Holy One,
I know what a gift it is
to step away from the ordinary
and listen for your voice
thrumming in my heart.

I follow the path of the mystics
who knew time apart
could open the heart in new ways.

Bless this time of retreat;
may it be a sacred pause
to refresh and restore me.
Infuse me once again
with a strong sense of your love.

May I open my heart
to holy surprise.
May I laugh freely with delight.

Magnify my silence
and let me see your shimmering presence
in every drop of dew, in each breath.
May every stone, leaf, and bird
point me closer to you.

Let me drink deeply from this well
and carry wisdom back into the world
like so much treasure.

TO KEEP HOPE ALIVE

Dream-Keeper,
bless me with vision
to see the possibilities
for this hurting and broken world.

Help me to remember
that hope is not a thing
but an action.
I cannot know that what I do
is of any consequence,
but I know I must do something.

Help me walk in trust
    that I plant seeds others will cultivate,
    that my kindness ripples out into the world,
    that justice is necessary,
    that joy is a sign of your presence,
    that love is at the foundation of everything.

On those days when hope
feels so far away,
surround me with kindred souls
who can help me trust in your goodness
when I must let go.

And on days
when my hope has been amplified,
buoyed by art, dreams, conversation,
let me carry it for others.

Sing to me of hope, Beloved,
and let me be a note in that melody.

FOR A WEDDING OR COMMITMENT CEREMONY

God of Abundant Love,
bless these two hearts
who step into a deeper union together
to become a radiant sign of love's call in the world.

Bless them in their sleeping under starlit skies
and dancing in light-filled days.
Bless them in the hurricanes of life
so that they may become shelter for each other.
May they play often, laugh daily,
hold each other closely.
May their differences become doorways
to insight and care.
May they have a community of love to support them.
Let them midwife one another in creative dreams.
May they see life as an unfolding adventure
and step into holy surprises while holding hands.

Bless the vows they made this day,
their words of promise like seeds ready to burst forth,
like the force of gravity drawing them always closer.

CONCLUSION

THREE PRACTICES

I close this book of blessings with an invitation into three practices that can deepen your experience of a spirituality of blessing and empower you to create your own blessings.

PRACTICE THE "SOAKING PRAYER"

I invite you to an adaptation of the practice of "soaking prayer," which is a way to simply "soak" in the presence of the divine, with no need to do anything, achieve anything, or figure things out.

Release your need to have anything happen during this prayer. Center yourself by connecting to your body and the sanctuary of your heart. Rest for a few moments in the presence of the Beloved.

Imagine yourself soaking in a warm body of water. Or if that image doesn't work for you, imagine being curled up in a warm blanket like a cocoon, with nowhere to go.

Soaking invites us to slow down, rest, be.

Imagine that you can see the blessings the Beloved showers upon you and creation as a warm golden light. Let this light intermingle with the waters or your cocoon so that you are bathing in its glow. Notice how you feel in your body.

From this place of soaking in blessing, call on this energy and send it to someone you love who is struggling. Wrap them in this care.

Draw this blessing into your being; let it shine a light on your gifts. See the Beloved blessing you in rest and in all you do.

Rest into a breathing prayer where, on the inhale, you draw into your being that energy of blessing and allow it to fill you and enliven you. On the exhale, send that energy of blessing out to the world, to touch all the places in need.

Release the prayer and return to the natural rhythm of your breath. Return gently to the room and consider drawing an image of your soaking prayer or writing down anything you want to remember.

PRACTICE BEING A BLESSING TO THE WORLD

I invite you into the practice of embodying your divinely bestowed gifts to become a blessing to others by the way you live and move and have your being.

Begin by centering yourself and letting your breath slow and deepen. Drop your awareness into the sanctuary of your heart. Rest for a few moments in the presence of the Beloved.

Call on the presence of Mary, the God-bearer, who calls us to birth the holy into the world and, through this, to be a blessing in all we do. She said her sacred yes without knowing all that would come as a result—sit with her in that uncertainty. How has her yes been a blessing to others?

Connect to your own deep desires of the heart. How do you long to be a blessing to the world? How is the holy being birthed in you?

Share this desire with Mary and ask her for any wisdom she has to offer.

Ask her to pray for you in the season ahead. With the eyes of your heart, imagine what it looks and feels like to use your gifts and circumstances to become a blessing to others.

Attend to how you feel in your body in response to this imagining. Notice if your body wants to take on a gesture or a shape in response. Adjust your posture and rest into it for a few moments. Return your awareness to the room and write down anything you want to remember.

Make a commitment to center yourself each morning in a prayer for blessing and a desire to become a blessing to others.

PRACTICE WRITING YOUR OWN BLESSINGS

I invite you to carry the spirit of blessing into everything you do with a writing exercise. Blessing is a way of holding a heart of gratitude for the multitude of gifts we experience moment by moment. Blessing means to make holy, but in this context, we are honoring the holiness already present in our activities and encounters. This writing practice is about naming God as already at work in myriad ways within and around us.

Consider writing a blessing for the creatures in your life, whether domesticated animals or wilder ones you encounter out in nature. Bless the unfolding rhythms of the day and the cathedrals of creation that inspire you. Bless the food you eat as nourishment from the earth to sustain your life and service.

Prepare for this practice by gathering a pen and paper in your prayer space.

Center yourself by becoming aware of your breath and dropping your awareness into the sanctuary of the heart. Rest for a few moments in the presence of the Beloved. Connect to our infinite source of blessing, allowing yourself to be held in God's love and care.

Call to mind and heart a person or a situation tugging at your heart, where you long to offer a prayer or response. This could be for yourself or another, or more broadly for a situation in the world or in nature.

Allow some time to notice any bodily sensations, any feelings, any images, and any memories that arise in connection with this intention.

What are your longings and desires for this person or situation?

Each of us has access to an infinite source of blessing in our hearts, for the Divine One is present within each of us.

Imagine you are drawing from this infinite well of blessing within you and showering it on the person or situation you are imagining.

Blessing another is an act of vulnerability and tenderness. Notice what arises in you: what you notice, what you feel, and what you see. Then write down any words or images that you want to remember. For anything that's been sparked in your heart, create space and write those down. You can scatter notes all over the page like seeds. You don't have to worry about writing anything formal as you begin gathering images.

Blessings often follow a rhythm of "May the divine bless you with . . ." See what emerges as a request and adapt the opening address with your own name for the sacred presence. Keep returning to this phrase if you feel stuck for words. Review the images and words you have recorded on the page for inspiration.

Take as long as you need to write your blessing. When it is complete, read it through and imagine the words traveling from your heart to surround this person or situation with blessing and love.

Rest there for a few moments.

Consider reading it aloud to see how the rhythm of words feels on your tongue and in your heart.

If you wrote it for a particular person, consider sharing your writing with them.

ACKNOWLEDGMENTS

I am forever grateful to my husband and life partner, John, for continuing to support me in my writing and ministry.

Special thanks to our community at Abbey of the Arts, where versions of several of these blessings initially appeared. Many of them were written in service to particular prayer cycles, services, and retreats, and I am profoundly grateful for our community that prays together with such depth and inspires me to write blessings to call on the Holy One for grace in all of life's moments.

I am always grateful to all at Ave Maria Press for their ongoing enthusiastic support of my writing and work. A special thank you to Josh Noem for his keen edits.

Credits

Some blessings have been previously published in other books by Christine Valters Paintner or in Abbey of the Arts prayer cycles.

The original versions of the following blessings were published in *A Different Kind of Fast* by Augsburg Fortress Publishers, 2024. Used by permission.

For the Gift of Rest
For Being Present to Each Moment
For Trust in Abundance
For Patience
To Embrace Holy Darkness

For Hope in Grief
For Courage to Befriend Death

The original version of "For the New Year" was published in *Give Me a Word* by Augsburg Fortress Publishers, 2025. Used by permission.

The original versions of the following blessings were published in *Birthing the Holy* by Ave Maria Press, 2022. Used by permission.
To Follow Mary as God-Bearer
On the Feast of the Annunciation

The original versions of the following blessings were published in *The Love of Thousands* by Ave Maria Press, 2023. Used by permission.
For Becoming Wise and Well
On the Feast of the Guardian Angels
On the Feast of All Saints
On the Feast of All Souls

The original versions of the following blessings were published in the *Monk in the World* prayer cycle by Abbey of the Arts. Used by permission.
For Silence and Solitude
For Creative Joy
For Bountiful Hospitality
For Inspiration to Begin Again

The original versions of the following blessings were published in the "Soul of a Pilgrim" prayer cycle by Abbey of the Arts. Used by permission.
For Saying Yes to the Journey
For Traveling Lightly

For Guidance on Our Way
For Beginning Again
For Stepping into the Unknown
For Coming Home

The original versions of the following blessings were published in the "Earth Monastery" prayer cycle by Abbey of the Arts. Used by permission.

For Kinship with Creation
For the Earth, Our Sanctuary
For Our Journey Through the Seasons
To Hear Our Calling Through Creation
For Learning from the Wisdom of Nature
A Lament for Creation
For Savoring the Wild Sacrament of Creation
A Song of Praise
To Be Blessed by the Gifts of the Elements

For more blessings not included here, check out Christine Valters Paintner's book on Mary titled Birthing the Holy *and her book on angels, saints, and ancestors titled* The Love of Thousands.

CHRISTINE VALTERS PAINTNER is the online abbess for Abbey of the Arts, a virtual monastery offering classes and resources on contemplative practice and creative expression. She earned a doctorate in Christian spirituality from the Graduate Theological Union in Berkeley, California, and achieved professional status as a registered expressive arts consultant and educator from the International Expressive Arts Therapy Association. She is also trained as a spiritual director and supervisor.

Paintner is the author of numerous spirituality titles, including *The Artist's Rule*; *A Midwinter God*; *The Love of Thousands*; *Birthing the Holy*; *Sacred Time*; *Earth, Our Original Monastery*; *The Soul's Slow Ripening*; *The Wisdom of the Body*; *Illuminating the Way*; *The Soul of a Pilgrim*; *Water, Wind, Earth, and Fire*; and three collections of poetry.

Paintner is a Benedictine oblate living in Galway, Ireland, with her husband, John. Together they lead online retreats on their website, abbeyofthearts.com.

Facebook: @abbeyofthearts
Instagram: @abbeyofthearts
YouTube: @abbeyofheartsireland

MORE BY
CHRISTINE VALTERS PAINTNER

Birthing the Holy
Wisdom from Mary to Nurture Creativity and Renewal

Earth, Our Original Monastery
Cultivating Wonder and Gratitude through Intimacy with Nature

Eyes of the Heart
Photography as a Christian Contemplative Practice

Illuminating the Way
Embracing the Wisdom of Monks and Mystics

A Midwinter God
Encountering the Divine in Seasons of Darkness

Sacred Time
Embracing an Intentional Way of Life

The Artist's Rule
Nurturing Your Creative Soul with Monastic Wisdom

The Soul of a Pilgrim
Eight Practices for the Journey Within

The Soul's Slow Ripening
12 Celtic Practices for Seeking the Sacred

The Wisdom of the Body
A Contemplative Journey to Wholeness for Women

Water, Wind, Earth, and Fire
The Christian Practice of Praying with the Elements